A Let's-Read-and-Find-Out Book™

Hear Your Heart

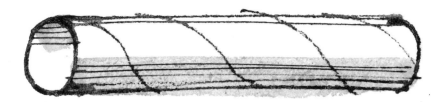

by *PAUL SHOWERS*

illustrated by *JOSEPH LOW*

A Harper Trophy Book

Harper & Row, Publishers

LET'S-READ-AND-FIND-OUT BOOKS™

The *Let's-Read-and-Find-Out Book*™ series was originated by Dr. Franklyn M. Branley, Astronomer Emeritus and former Chairman of the American Museum-Hayden Planetarium, and was formerly co-edited by him and Dr. Roma Gans, Professor Emeritus of Childhood Education, Teachers College, Columbia University. Text and illustrations for each of the more than 100 books in the series are checked for accuracy by an expert in the relevant field. The titles available in paperback are listed below. Look for them at your local bookstore or library.

Hear Your Heart
Text copyright © 1968 by Paul Showers
Illustrations copyright © 1968 by Joseph Low
Printed in the U.S.A. All rights reserved.

Library of Congress Catalog Card Number: 85-43026
Trade ISBN 0-690-37378-3
Library ISBN 0-690-37379-1
Trophy ISBN 0-06-445007-4
First Harper Trophy edition, 1985.
Published in hardcover by Thomas Y. Crowell

Hear Your Heart

Every time I go to the doctor, he listens to my chest.

He wants to hear how my heart beats.

He listens with his stethoscope.

He puts a little round button on my chest and listens.

The button is cold. It makes me shiver.

I like my stethoscope much better. It isn't cold.
My stethoscope is a cardboard tube.
I listen to hearts with it.
My sister Lisa has one, too. We listen to each other's
  heart.

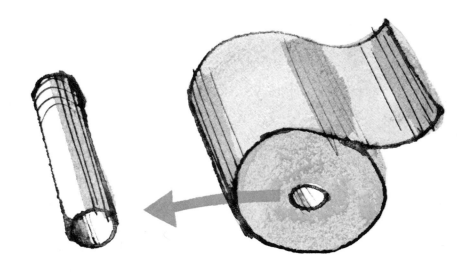

Sometimes we use tubes from old rolls of paper towels.

Sometimes we even use tubes from old toilet-paper
  rolls. Any kind of cardboard tube will do.

This is how you do it.

Ask your friend to find the spot on his chest where
  he can feel his heart beating.

Put one end of your tube against this spot.

Now listen at the other end.

We listen to our friends' hearts,
   and they listen to ours.
Phil's heart beats like this:
     pum-pum pum-pum pum-pum pum-pum.
Molly's heart beats the same way.
So does mine. So does Lisa's.

My father's heart is slower. It beats like this:
ka dum   ka dum   ka dum   ka dum.

Andrew is only eleven months old.
Mother holds him, and we listen to his heart.
Andrew's heart has a very quick beat. It goes:
tuppa tuppa tuppa tuppa tuppa.

Put your hand on your chest.

Can you feel your heart?

It is working. Your heart is moving blood through
your body.

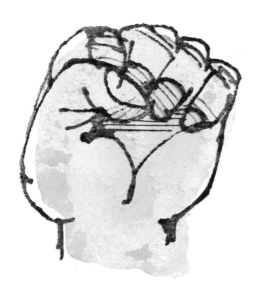

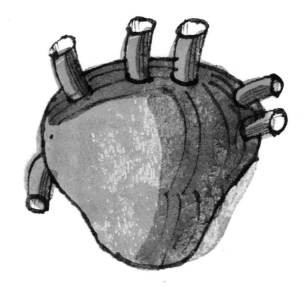

Your heart is about as big as your fist.
It doesn't look like a heart on a valentine.
It looks more like a pear from a pear tree.
Your heart has tubes attached to it.
Blood flows in and out of your heart
through these tubes.

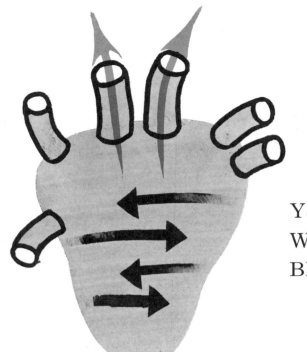

Your heart is full of blood.
When it beats, it squeezes itself together.
Blood squirts out into some of the tubes.

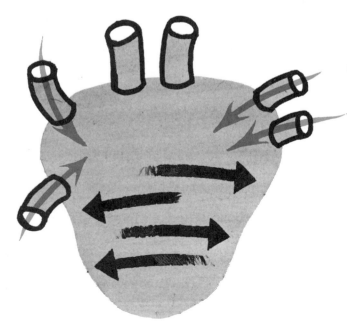

Then your heart stops squeezing
and opens up again.

Blood comes into it
through the other tubes.

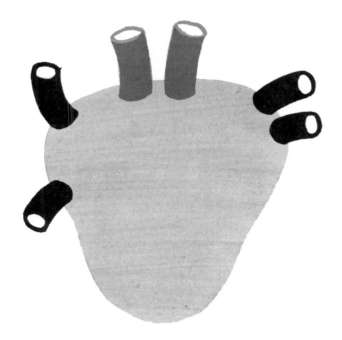

The tubes that lead the blood away from your heart
   are called arteries.
The tubes that bring the blood into your heart are
   called veins.
In this picture, the arteries are colored red.
The veins are black.

Your heart is made of strong muscle.

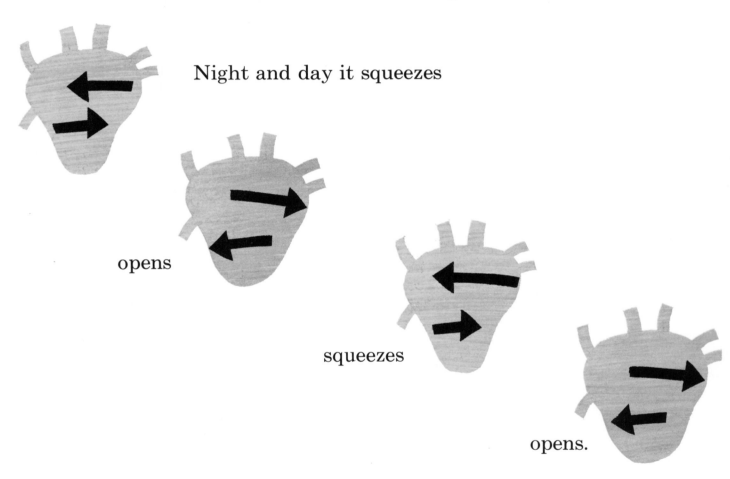

Night and day it squeezes

opens

squeezes

opens.

It beats all the time.

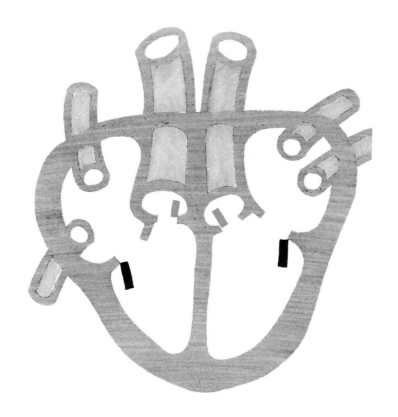

A heart is something like this inside:

It is divided down the middle into two halves.

Each half has veins and an artery attached to it.

Each half has little doors in it, too.

These doors are called valves.

In this drawing the valves are colored red and black.

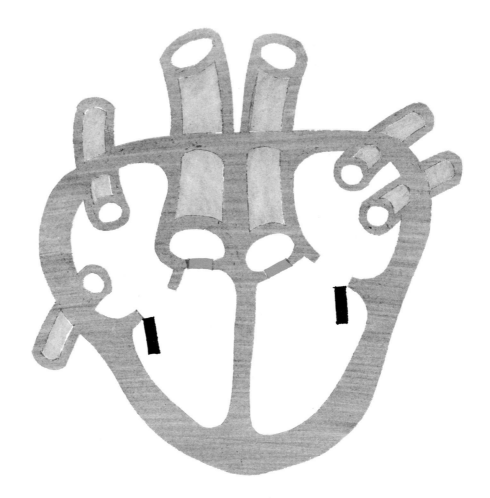

All day long, all night long, these valves
open and close,
open and close.
When the black valves open, the red valves close.

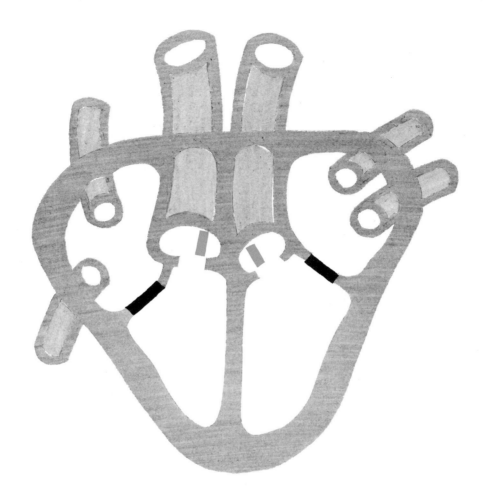

When the red valves open, the black valves close.

The valves keep the blood moving in the right direction—

    IN from the veins,

    OUT through the arteries.

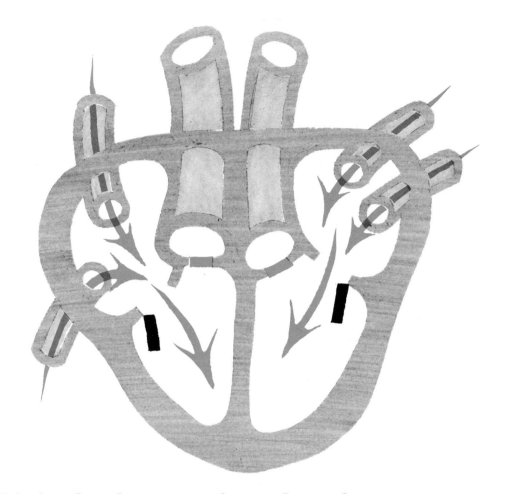

This is what happens when a heart beats:

Each half works the same way.

First, blood comes in from the big veins at the top of the heart.

The black valves are open. The blood moves down through them.

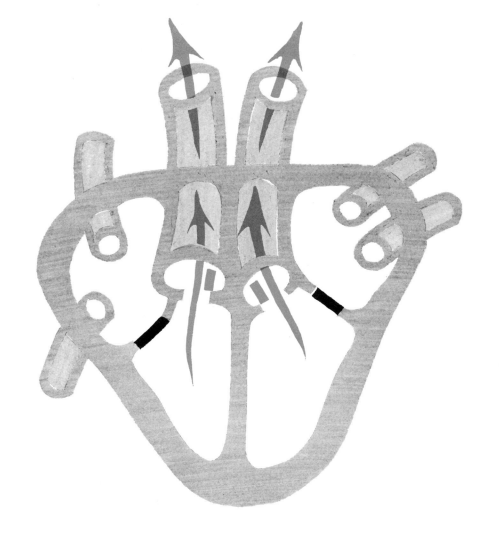

Then the heart squeezes. It gives the blood a push.
The black valves close. The red valves open.
Blood cannot flow back into the veins.
It can only flow out into the arteries.

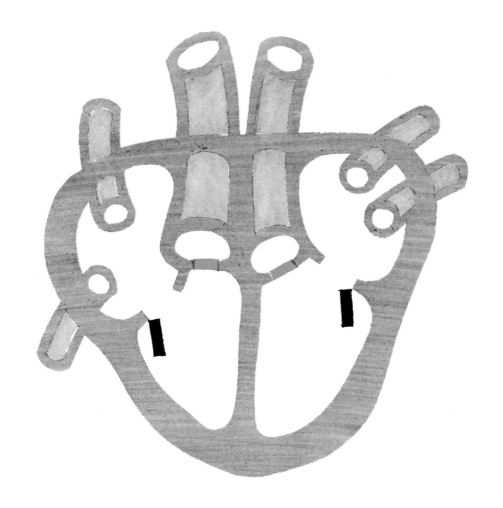

The heart stops squeezing and opens up again.
The black valves open; the red valves snap shut.

The blood in the arteries cannot flow back into the heart.

Only the blood in the veins can come in through the black valves.

Once more the heart fills with blood.

Once more it is ready to squeeze blood out into the arteries.

Big arteries spread out from your heart.

They go to your arms and legs and head.

Smaller arteries branch out from the big ones.

They branch out to the top of your head—

to the tips of your fingers

to the tips of your toes

to every part of your body.

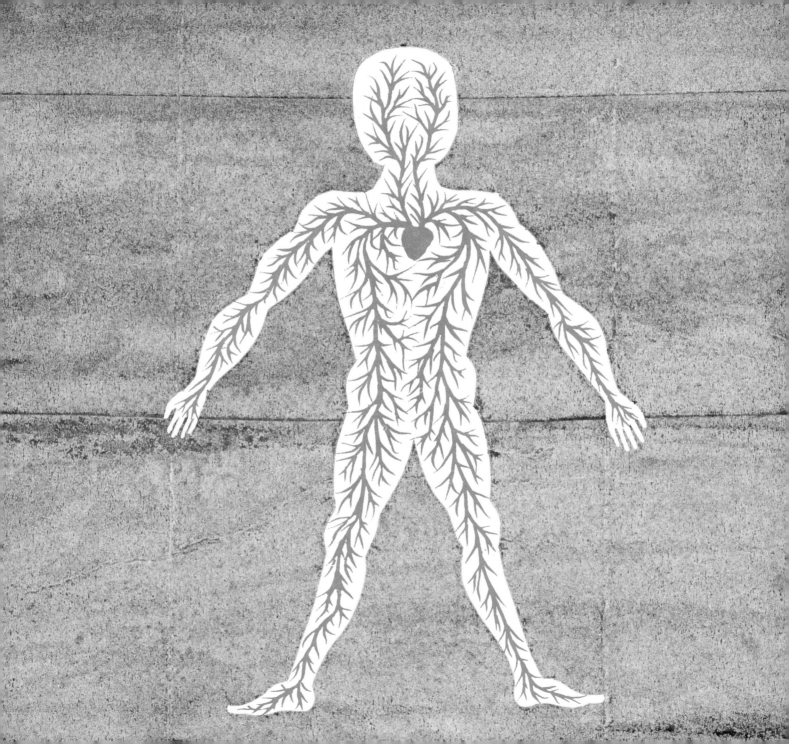

Touch your wrist just below your thumb.
Press gently with your fingertips.

Do you feel something push against your fingers?
push   push   push.

This is called your pulse.

You are feeling a small artery in your wrist.
Your heart is pushing blood through it:
   beat—push   beat—push   beat—push.

You can tell how fast your heart is beating
by feeling your pulse.

You can feel the pulse in other arteries in your body.
Touch your temples.
They are on either side of your head between your
    eyes and ears.
There is an artery in each temple. Can you feel it?

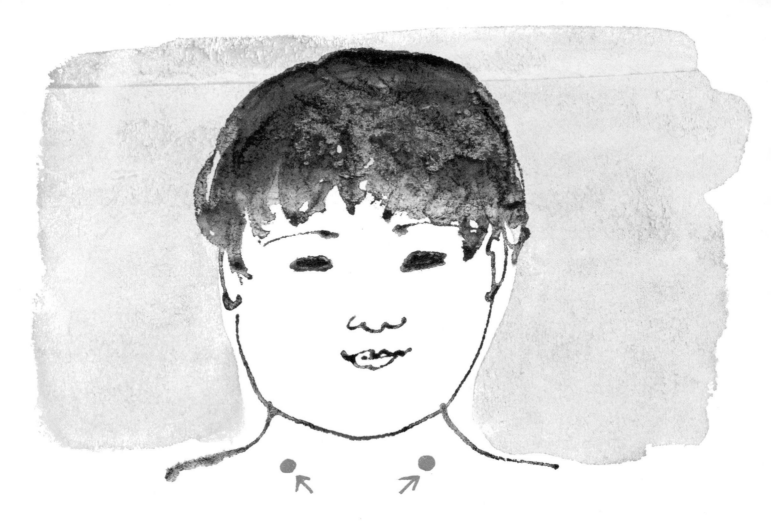

Touch the sides of your neck
 just below your chin
 or down where it joins your body.
Touch lightly. Can you feel the arteries pulsing there?

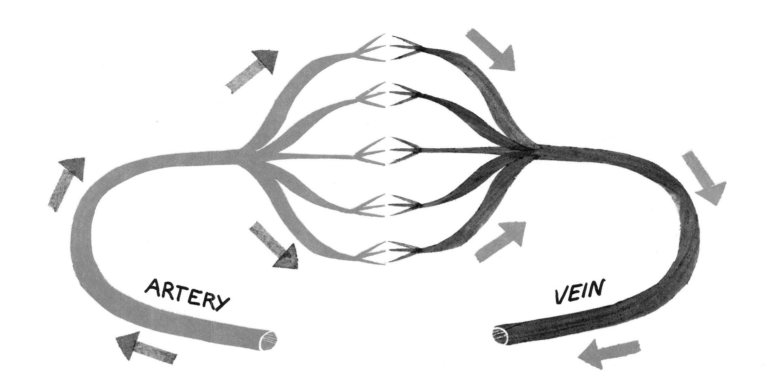

Blood moves out from your heart through your
   arteries.

It reaches every part of your body.

When it reaches the very smallest arteries,
   the blood passes into tubes that carry it back to
   the heart.

These tubes are called veins.

The tiny veins run into bigger veins.

They are like brooks
    that flow into streams
        that flow into rivers.

There are veins on the back of my hand.
They are too small to see.

But I can see the veins on the back of my father's
    hands.

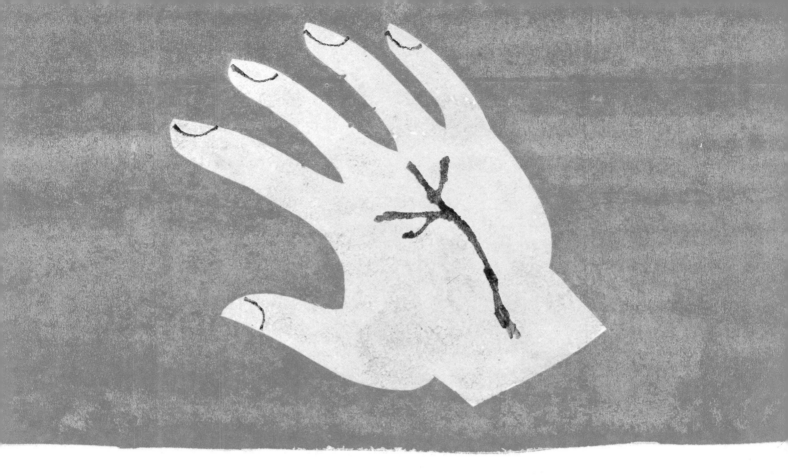

They are just under the skin.

They are big and full of blood. They make the skin
  stick out.

When you touch a vein, you cannot feel a pulse.

You can feel a pulse only in an artery.

The pulse tells how fast the heart is beating.
How fast is your heart beating
right now as you read this book?
Get a watch with a second hand and count your pulse.
How many times does your heart beat in one minute?

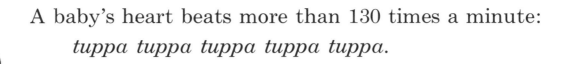

A baby's heart beats more than 130 times a minute:
tuppa tuppa tuppa tuppa tuppa.

A man's heart beats about 72 times a minute:
ka dum   ka dum   ka dum   ka dum.

The heart of an eight-year-old boy beats about
90 times a minute:
pum-pum   pum-pum   pum-pum   pum-pum.
Sometimes it goes a little faster,
sometimes a little slower.

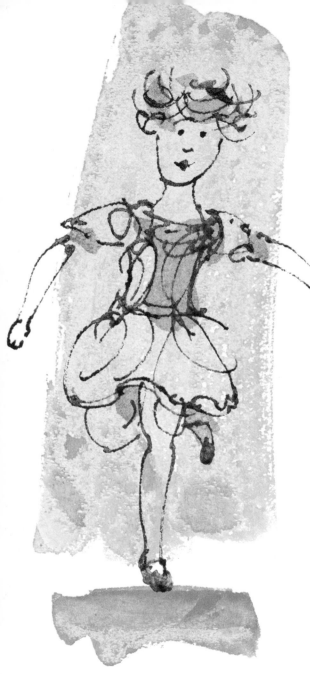

Your heart beats faster when you exercise.
Try this and see for yourself.

Hop up and down on one foot
twenty times.

Now sit down and feel your pulse.

Watch the second hand of your watch.

Count.

How fast is your heart beating now?

Your heart beats faster when you run

or jump.

When you sleep, it beats much slower.

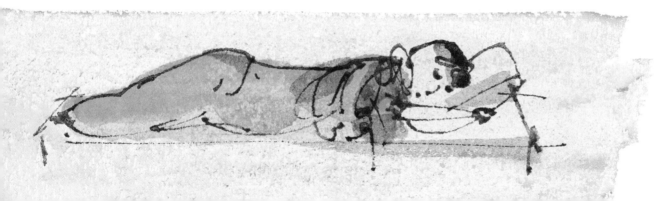

A big animal's heart beats more slowly than a little animal's.

An elephant's heart beats only 20 to 25 times a minute.

A mouse's heart beats more than 500 times a minute.

Lisa has a parakeet named Clarence.
When we hold Clarence, we can feel his heart beating.
His heart goes like this:
pat-pat-pat-pat-pat.
It beats so fast we can't keep count.

Your heart works all the time:

squeeze—open squeeze—open squeeze—open

No other part of your body works so hard.

Your hand is strong, but not so strong as your heart.

Try this:

Open your hand. Close it in a fist.

Open it. Close it.

How long can you keep doing this?

How long before your hand gets tired?

Your heart never gets tired.
It takes a little rest after each beat.
But it doesn't stop beating.

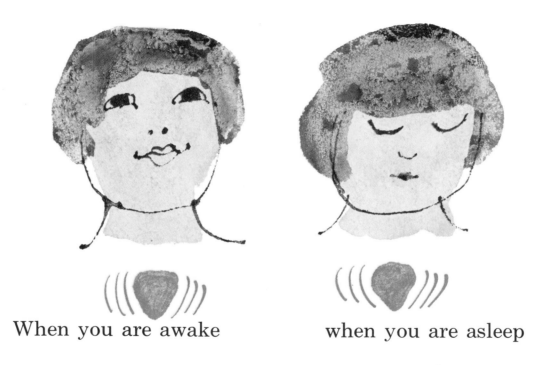

When you are awake   when you are asleep

beat—push beat—push beat—push.

Your heart keeps moving the blood through your body.

ABOUT THE AUTHOR

Paul Showers is a newspaperman and writer. His first job was with the Detroit *Free Press;* later he worked on the New York *Herald Tribune.* During World War II he served in the Air Corps for a year, then joined the staff of *Yank,* the Army weekly. Since the war, with the exception of a brief stint with the New York *Sunday Mirror,* he has been a member of *The New York Times* Sunday department staff.

Mr. Showers was born in Sunnyside, Washington, received his B.A. degree from the University of Michigan, and now lives in California.

ABOUT THE ARTIST

Joseph Low was born in Coraopolis, Pennsylvania; he attended schools in Oak Park, Illinois, and studied at the University of Illinois. Finding that he could pursue his own artistic interests by studying independently in museums and libraries, Mr. Low concentrated on the graphic arts; he taught himself the skills that he needed and acquired the necessary tools.

After spending some time at the Art Student's League in New York City, Joseph Low taught graphic arts at Indiana University for three years. He is not only an artist but also a printer and publisher with his own Eden Hill Press.

His work has been exhibited in museums across the United States, in England, in South America, in the Orient, and in Europe. He and his wife live in Connecticut in a house overlooking Long Island Sound and the Norwalk Islands, a ten-minute walk from their boat, a midget ocean racer.